W9-DIE-995

59n
Far

Library of Congress Cataloging-in-Publication Data

Farré, Marie
    (Young Discovery Library; 1)
    Translation of: Qui a peur des crocodiles?
    Includes index.
    Summary: Describes the physical characteristics, behavior,
    and peculiar habits of crocodiles, including how to distinguish
    them from alligators.
    1. Crocodiles — Juvenile literature. 2. Alligators — Juvenile
    literature. [1. Crocodiles] I. Wallis, Diz, ill. II. Title
    III. Series: Young Discovery Library (Series); 1.
QL666.C925F3713   1988   597.98   87-31804
ISBN 0-944589-01-4

CHILDRENS PRESS CHOICE

A Young Discovery Library title selected for educational distribution

ISBN 0-516-08271-X

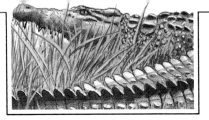

Written by Marie Farré
Illustrated by Diz Wallis

Specialist Adviser:
Dr. Donald Bruning
New York Zoological Society

ISBN 0-944589-01-4
First U.S. Publication 1988 by
Young Discovery Library
217 Main St. • Ossining, NY 10562

©1985 by Editions Gallimard
Translated by Sarah Matthews
English text © 1986 by Moonlight Publishing Ltd.
Thanks to Aileen Buhl

YOUNG DISCOVERY LIBRARY

Crocodiles and Alligators

Once upon a time,
   crocodiles fed on cakes and honey...

YOUNG DISCOVERY LIBRARY

In ancient Egypt, crocodiles were worshipped as gods. At the time of the Pharaohs a whole city, called Crocodilopis, was built in their honor.

The crocodile god was called Sebek.

The crocodiles lived in a sacred lake. Their priests put gold bracelets on their arms, and fed them on cakes and honey.

Crocodile mummy

When a crocodile died, the priests mummified it. They dried the body and wrapped it in herbs and bandages so that it did not rot.

Have you seen a crocodile?

They don't look
very fierce
lying in the zoo.
But in the wild no
creature dares attack
a full-grown crocodile —
except man. They live
beside lakes and rivers in Africa,
Asia, Australia and parts of America.

Crocodiles are reptiles...

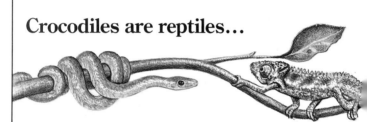

like snakes...
tortoises...
lizards.
They have dry,
scaly skin and
lay eggs on land.

They are the most powerful reptiles in the world.

Crocodiles have lived in the world since
the time of the dinosaurs.

A time when reptiles
ruled the world.

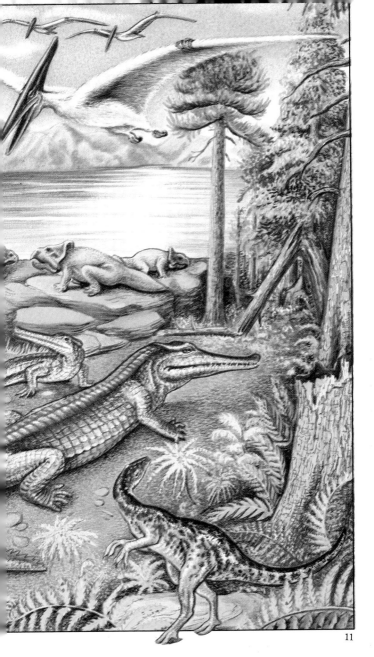

Crocodiles have several close relatives: alligators, cayman, gharials.

Nile crocodile

How can you tell if it's a crocodile?
By the fourth tooth which sticks out on each side of the lower jaw.

Or a cayman?
They have a black crest between their eyes.

Central American cayman

Or an alligator? Their heads are broad, and their fourth tooth does not stick out.

Or a gharial?
By its long, narrow jaw, which helps it catch fish to eat.

◀ Mississippi alligator

Indian ▶ gharial

The noise a crocodile makes is called a bellow, though it sounds more like a groan. Did you know that there are some crocodiles which are four times as big as you are, and over forty times heavier?

A crocodile's skin is as tough as armor.

It is made of scales. But it's not stiff like tortoiseshell. The scales fit beside each other and the skin moves and bends easily.

A crocodile has sharp claws on its feet. The scales on its tail stand up to form a spiky ridge.

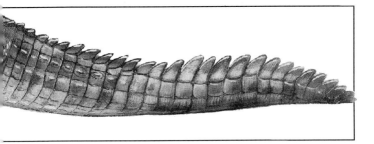

A crocodile can see at night like a cat. The pupils of its eyes get wider in the dark.

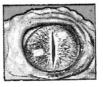

In daylight

At night

What are its weapons?

Its powerful tail and its strong jaws. A crocodile has a lot of teeth. They come out easily, but when one falls out, another one grows in its place straight away. A tooth can be renewed 45 times.

They have a piece of stretchy skin at the corners of their mouths so that they can open them very wide.

The nest is shaped like a deep basket.

How are crocodiles born?

In the spring, the mother crocodile digs a nest with her front legs. In the nest she lays about fifty leathery white eggs, the size of hens' eggs. Then she covers the nest with sand.

Watch out! A lot of animals love to eat crocodiles' eggs!

While the eggs are incubating, the mother hardly leaves the nest. If the weather is hot, she scurries down to the water for a dip, then lies over the nest to cool it down.

Monitor lizards are very crafty. While the male lures the crocodile away from the nest. the female eats the eggs.

When the eggs are
ready to hatch, after
nine or ten weeks, the baby
crocodiles call out from
inside the eggs. While their mother
scrapes the sand
from the nest, they
break out of the eggs,
using a special **egg
tooth** which drops
off after they have
hatched.

A baby crocodile is
the size of a small lizard.

The dash for the water

As soon as they are out of the egg, the
babies head for the water. They know
how to swim immediately! Sometimes
their mother carries them down to the
water in her mouth.

Baby crocodiles eat
small worms, snails and insects.

Do all baby crocodiles grow up?

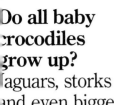

One baby cayman the less...

Jaguars, storks and even bigger crocodiles enjoy eating them. So the young crocodiles have a special nursery area, with holes in the riverbank to hide in, where they can grow up safely. Despite all this care, though, only about two crocodiles from each clutch of eggs survive long enough to lay eggs themselves. But these two may live at least fifty years.

At 7 years old, it is an adult.

A crocodile swims by moving its tail. Only its eyes, ears and nostrils show above the water!

Why do crocodiles sleep in the water?

Like all reptiles, crocodiles lose their body heat when the temperature goes down. But water keeps the sun's heat longer than the air, so crocodiles stay all night in the warm water and only crawl out at dawn when the water is becoming cooler, and the sun has risen. They lie in its warmth on the bank.

A crocodile can stay underwater for up to two hours.

It can close its nostrils, then the water cannot get in. It has a special transparent eyelid so that it can see underwater. Its ears are protected underwater too, by a

 thin skin which stops water getting in, but still lets sound through.

What animals do crocodiles attack?

Big animals such as buffalo, zebra, gazelle, smaller animals like hyena — sometimes they even attack elephants, but they only manage to bite their noses. When they get old, crocodiles may be eaten themselves, by other crocodiles.

Do they eat often?

A crocodile can go two or three months without eating if it has to.

A dozen crocodiles can kill and eat a hippo.

Crocodiles are cunning hunters.

You can see how a crocodile hunts a gazelle. After lying in ambush, it knocks the gazelle into the water with its tail, and jumps in after it, catching one of its legs in its mouth. It pulls the gazelle under and drowns it. It tears bits off by twisting over and over. The pieces must be swallowed whole as a crocodile can't chew.

Did you know that a crocodile swallows pebbles?

It may do this because the small stones help to break up the food which the crocodile has gulped down.

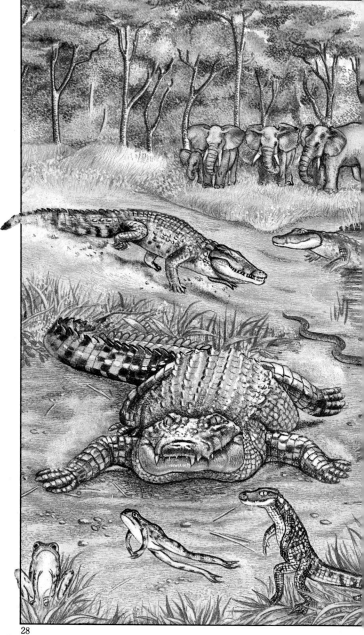

After it has eaten, the crocodile will lie and rest on the bank in the sun. If it gets too hot it will open its mouth and let the evaporation om the damp skin inside cool it down. r it might burrow into the cool mud.

ow do crocodiles move on land?
hey crawl or trot, or sometimes, on wet ass, they glide, pushing themselves ong with their tails.

If, one day, you find yourself being chased by a crocodile, run in zigzags. Crocodiles can't turn easily, and this slows them down.

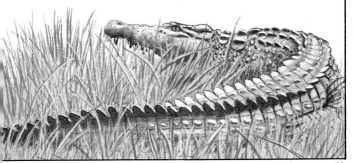

Two crocodiles snort warnings at each other.

Each group has its own territory.

Crocodiles usually
live in groups. The
boundaries of
their territory
are marked by
the males with a
stong smell of musk,
produced by a gland
under their bellies.

They bite each
other and thrash
with their tails.

Everyone knows his place.

The leader has the best spot on the
riverbank, the greatest number of
females, the biggest bits of meat. Old
crocodiles lie on the soft grass, the
younger ones have to make do with the
sloping banks.

The loser lifts his
muzzle to show he's
beaten, and then makes off.

Do crocodiles really cry?

If you pretend to be sad, people may say you're crying crocodile tears. But crocodiles only have tears in their eyes if they yawn, or, if they've been in the sea, to wash the salt out.

Crocodiles have the strangest toothbrushes!

They are birds: **plovers.** They peck off the leeches and the bits of food that get stuck between the crocodile's teeth.

Spur-winged plovers

help the crocodile in a different way by eating the ticks that live between his scales.

When danger comes near, the plovers cry out, and the crocodiles all dive underwater.

These animals, on Earth since prehistoric times, are dying out.
Man has almost destroyed them. Their skins are valuable, and they used to be hunted for them, by men with guns. Nowadays we are beginning to realize that crocodiles are precious and irreplaceable. They are protected and live in reserves. The skin used for expensive handbags, belts and shoes comes from crocodiles raised on special farms. The musk is used in perfumes.

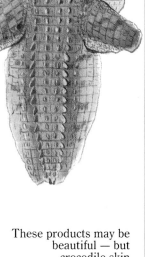

These products may be beautiful — but crocodile skin looks better on crocodiles.

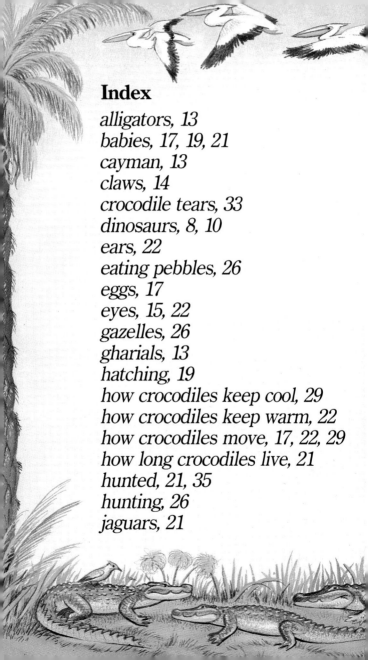

Index

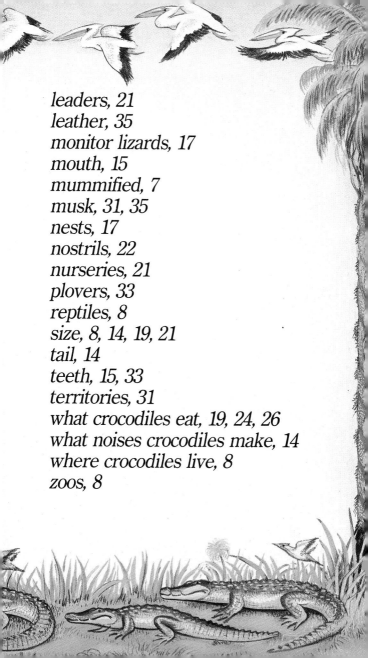

The Crocodile

How doth the little crocodile
  Improve his shining tail,
And pour the waters of the Nile
  On every golden scale!

How cheerfully he seems to grin!
  How neatly spread his claws,
And welcomes little fishes in
  With gently smiling jaws!

Lewis Carroll